First published in 2015 by Wayland
Text copyright © Pat Thomas 2015
Illustrations copyright © Wayland 2015

Dewey number: 155.2'32-dc23
ISBN: 978 0 7502 8957 3
Library eBook ISBN: 978 0 7502 8795 1

10 9 8 7 6 5 4 3 2 1

MIX
Paper from
responsible sources
FSC® C104740
FSC
www.fsc.org

Concept design: Kate Buxton
Series design: Paul Cherrill for Basement68
Editor: Victoria Brooker

Printed in China

Wayland, an imprint of Hachette Children's Group
Part of Hodder & Stoughton
Carmelite House, 50 Victoria Embankment
London EC4Y 0DZ

An Hachette UK Company
www.hachette.co.uk
www.hachettechildrens.co.uk

Leave Me Alone!

A FIRST LOOK AT SHYNESS

PAT THOMAS
ILLUSTRATED BY CLAIRE KEAY

WAYLAND

Do you ever feel shy?

Everyone has that feeling at some time in
their lives – even grown-ups!

Shyness is a feeling – it's kind of like being scared and worried all at the same time.

When you are feeling shy, it's easy to think that nobody likes you or cares about you, or wants to make friends with you – even though that's not true.

When you are feeling shy you worry a lot about what others think of you and it can be hard to join in with groups or just talk or laugh with the people around you.

What about you?

Are you sometimes shy?

What sort of things do you worry about?

Feeling shy can tie your tummy up in knots and make you feel afraid of new places and people.

And it can make you want to hide
away and be on your own.

Sometimes it can be nice to just play on your own and not have to talk to anyone or share your things.

But being on your own all the time can also make you feel lonely and left out.

And some things are just more fun when there are two or more of you together.

Sometimes feeling shy can even
be a good thing. Shy people
often think twice before
doing something.

That can help keep you out of trouble!

But when you are feeling really worried, talking to your parents, carers or teachers about how you feel is a good way to help you feel safer and more confident.

Whatever size we are, we all have special talents and skills – being overweight doesn't change that.

ART CUP

What about you?

What sorts of things are you good at? What do you enjoy doing? Are there any new things you'd like to try?

Sometimes when you are overweight people will try to make you feel bad about it.

They may try to stop you from sitting next to them or playing games with them...

...or tease or bully you because you are not the same as them. Teasing or bullying people for how they look is mean and is never the right thing to do.

People who are overweight
are not greedy or lazy.

Often they just need someone like their
friends or family or teachers to help them learn
how to take care of themselves by eating
less and exercising more.

Learning to eat the right foods, to stop eating when you are full and to exercise more, is like learning to do anything else.

It takes practice and patience and you need lots of people around you who can help you to get better at it.

If you have friends or other members of your family that are overweight you can all practise together...

...and help each other to say 'no thank you' to foods that look nice, but which aren't very good for you.

It's much easier to stay healthy when we all help and support each other.

Your body can do amazing things
and take you to amazing places
if you take care of it.

Eating just the right amount
of healthy food is a good way to
make sure you enjoy yourself
along the way.

HOW TO USE THIS BOOK

The purpose of this book is to help parents and young children have their first discussions about food and health. Children have to learn about healthy eating the same way they have to learn about other things - through repetition and positive reinforcement. The questions in the "What about you?" sections can be useful prompts for understanding things from your child's point of view.

Parents are in charge. Young children do not make independent decisions about what to eat, or how much to eat, or when to eat. Nor are they in charge of their own social and exercise schedules. Very few children can lose weight without parental support, so do what you can to help set in stone healthy habits that will last a lifetime.

Choose your words carefully. Emotionally charged discussions about weight aren't appropriate at any time, but in young children they risk making them far too self-conscious. Very young children are generally not too concerned with what they look like until someone tells them otherwise. Focus on positives, for instance on the ways that healthy food makes you feel stronger and makes your brain smarter.

Put it in context. Instead of big overwhelming conversations – use time together, for instance, when food shopping to casually discuss why you are choosing one food over another, or the health benefits of certain foods.

Sensible portions. For very young children, sensible portions of healthy foods is the best way to begin to manage weight problems. Use this book to help them understand the concept of 'enough' and how it can help them feel better and have more energy.

It's a family affair. Children imitate their parents' eating and exercise habits and being overweight does tend to run in families.

To encourage your child to get up and move, make getting healthy a family project where everyone can join in. Special activities just for kids, such as the Saturday gym or swimming, are great. But regular activities that all the family can enjoy are also a good way of encouraging your child to value being active.

Cut TV time. Reducing the amount of time your child spends watching TV has two big benefits. It helps direct them into more active pastimes and it also reduces their exposure to TV commercials for unhealthy foods. Studies show that commercials have a big influence on children's eating habits. When watching TV you can help by discussing why certain foods are not healthy and why you don't buy them for your family.

Healthy snacks. Children need to eat. Unless advised by a medical professional for a pressing health reason, young children should not diet and snacks should not be denied them if they are genuinely hungry. Make sure you have healthy snacks like fruit or vegetables on hand at home. Likewise some schools have found that introducing a "fruit time" in the afternoon is a great time to talk about healthy foods and their effects on the body - for instance how fruit or vegetables can improve energy levels and help to reinforce good eating habits.

Schools projects. Schools are well placed to teach about diet and fitness from many different angles – and to enforce a zero tolerance policy on bullying and teasing. Exploring the foods people from other cultures consider healthy can broaden children's horizons considerably. Class projects on food and portion sizes is also important. Similarly introducing a wide range of PE or playground activities can aid children in finding a sport which suits them.

BOOKS TO READ

For children

Hamster Camp: How Harry Got Fit
Teresa Bateman
(Albert Whitman & Company, 2005)

Healthy and Happy: Eating Well
Robyn Hardyman
(Wayland, 2011)

Looking After Me: Eating Well
Liz Gogerly and Mike Gordon
(Wayland, 2013)

Mini and Me: Learning Healthy Habits
Shelly Stockum, Sandi Stewart, Greg Stockum
(Jabberwocky Books, 2009)

For parents

Your Child's Weight: Helping Without Harming
Ellyn Satter
(Kelcy Press, 2005)

Red Light, Green Light, Eat Right: The Food Solution That Let's Kids Be Kids
Joanna Dolgoff
(Rodale Books, 2009)

How to Raise a Healthy Child in Spite of Your Doctor
Robert Mendelsohn
(Ballantine Books Inc, 1987)

RESOURCES FOR ADULTS

www.cdc.gov/healthyweight/children/

Advice for parents on how to help overweight children.

www.nhs.uk/change4life/Pages/change-for-life.aspx

A website giving advice for on how to start eating healthily and getting more exercise for families.

www.webmd.com/parenting/raising-fit-kids/weight/safe-weight-loss

A WebMD resource to help families make sensible changes that benefit overweight children.